Down to a Sunless Sea

The Strange World of Hydrothermal Vents

Kate Madin

RSVP ®

RAINTREE
STECK-VAUGHN
P U B L I S H E R S
A Steck-Vaughn Company

Austin, Texas

www.steck-vaughn.com

To the memory of
Holger Jannasch (1924–1998)
and to all vent researchers

Steck-Vaughn Company

First published 2000 by Raintree Steck-Vaughn Publishers,
an imprint of Steck-Vaughn Company.

Library of Congress Cataloging-in-Publication Data

Madin, Kate.
      Down to a sunless sea: the strange world of hydrothermal vents/Kate Madin.
          p. cm— (Turnstone ocean explorer book)
      Includes bibliographical references.
      Summary: Explains the nature and discovery of hydrothermal vents, the animals that
live there, and current studies about these underwater environments.
      ISBN 0-7398-1238-6 (hardcover) ISBN 0-7398-1239-4 (softcover)
      1. Hydrothermal vent animals—Juvenile literature. 2. Hydrothermal vents—Juvenile
literature. [1. Hydrothermal vents. 2. Hydrothermal vent ecology. 3. Marine animals.
4. Ecology.]
I. Title. II. Series: Turnstone ocean explorer book.
QL 125.6.M33 1999   99-28962
591.77'9—dc21   CIP

For information about this and other Turnstone reference books and educational materials,
visit Turnstone Publishing Group on the World Wide Web at http://turnstonepub.com.

Photo credits listed on page 64 constitute part of this copyright page.

Printed and bound in the United States of America.

1 2 3 4 5 6 7 8 9 0 LB 04 03 02 01 00 99

CONTENTS

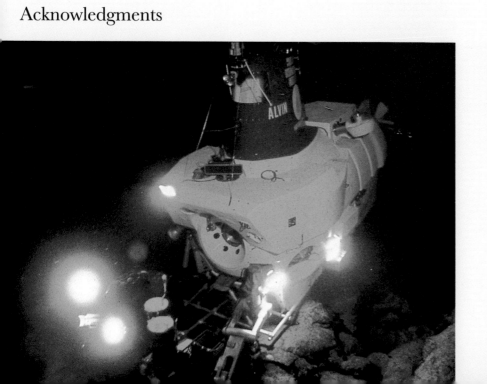

1

DISCOVERY!

"[This is] one of the major biological discoveries of the twentieth century."
—Biologist Holger Jannasch on the discovery of hydrothermal vents

(above)
Twenty years ago, less than one percent of the seafloor had been visited by people. Even today, vast areas of seafloor remain unexplored. Most of the ocean floor that has been explored looks bare, like this.

(left)
The discovery of fountains of hot water opened up a whole new world for scientists to investigate.

Thick darkness is all around. The temperature is just above freezing. Enormous pressure pushes on everything. A ridge of black rock leads to rounded rocks and stacks of stone. Smoky clouds rise many meters above tall stone chimneys. Some clouds are white; others are black with sooty particles that rain down from them. The water shimmers, and the rising clouds make currents swirl. Sticklike white creatures that look like bamboo with red crowns grow near cracks in the towers. Huge, white shells litter the nearby rocky ground. Other creatures swim through the rising clouds.

These smoking chimneys lie on the seafloor, about two and one-half kilometers (about one and one-half miles) under the ocean's surface. Here the water pressure is crushing. Clouds of hot fluid, some much hotter than a pot of boiling water (100°C, or 212°F), pour from the cracks in the rocks. Strange animals live here. This is a place people hadn't imagined could exist on Earth.

The place is part of the Mid-Ocean Ridge system, a chain of connected volcanic mountain ranges under Earth's oceans. Scientists have studied these areas since 1968, but before 1977 no human eyes had ever seen the fountains of hot fluid surrounded by odd animals.

5

The volcanic mountain ranges of the Mid-Ocean Ridge divide Earth's surface into sections called plates. At the edges of the plates, there is great deal of volcanic activity. Lava erupts, hardens, and becomes new crust. The plates move apart slowly in a process called seafloor spreading. One area where the seafloor is spreading is the Galápagos Rift, in the eastern Pacific Ocean near the Galápagos Islands. There, on a warm winter's day in 1977, the research ship *Lulu* slowed its engines and then stopped.

On the ship was a group of geologists, scientists who study Earth and its history, and geochemists, scientists who study the chemicals that make up the earth and the sea. They had come to study rocks and the seafloor. They also hoped to find a hydrothermal vent, where warm water rises out of the ocean floor like an underwater hot spring. They would explore the seafloor in *Alvin*, a deep-sea submersible that would dive about 2,500 meters (about 8,200 feet) deep.

From studying the work of many geologists around the world, the scientists knew that seawater sinks through cracks in the seafloor. Far beneath the crust, seawater is heated and picks up chemicals and minerals from the rocks that surround it. The scientists believed this hot, mineral-filled seawater returns from beneath the seafloor at a vent. Although they thought this was likely, no one had ever seen it happen. The Galápagos Rift seemed to be a perfect place to find a vent.

But the Galápagos Rift is big, and no one was sure hydrothermal vents

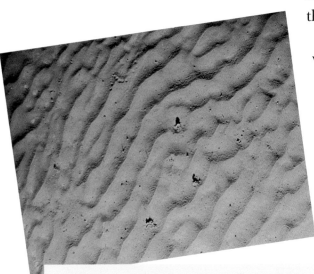

Welcome to the Bottom of the World

Air, light, and warmth surround us on land. The bottom of the ocean is a different world—dark and cold. Sunlight is made of different wavelengths of light (seen as colors in a rainbow). Water absorbs some wavelengths better than others, so colors disappear at different depths. Water absorbs less blue light than any other wavelength. That's why underwater pictures often look blue. But at about 120 meters (about 400 feet) deep, there's not enough blue light left for human eyes to see. No light reaches the deep ocean at all.

Temperature drops off quickly with depth. Though in many places the ocean's surface may be warm, from about 10°C (50°F) to 26.5°C (80°F), the temperature below 1,000 meters (about 3,300 feet) is between 5°C (41°F) and 2°C (35.6°F).

The Drifting World

Our globe is not what it seems on the surface. From space it looks like bits of high ground surrounded by a giant pool of water. Yet there are surprises at the bottom of the pool. A 64,000-kilometer (about 40,000-mile) mountain range called the Mid-Ocean Ridge circles our planet underwater, like seams that stitch the globe together.

The continents sit on top of plates that ride, or "float," on top of molten rock called magma. In a volcanic eruption, magma pushes up and out from cracks in the earth's crust. Under the sea, this volcanic activity causes eruptions that add new lava, or hardened magma, at the edges of the plates. The sections of seafloor move apart slowly. The edges of these sections where plates move apart are where hydrothermal vents can be found.

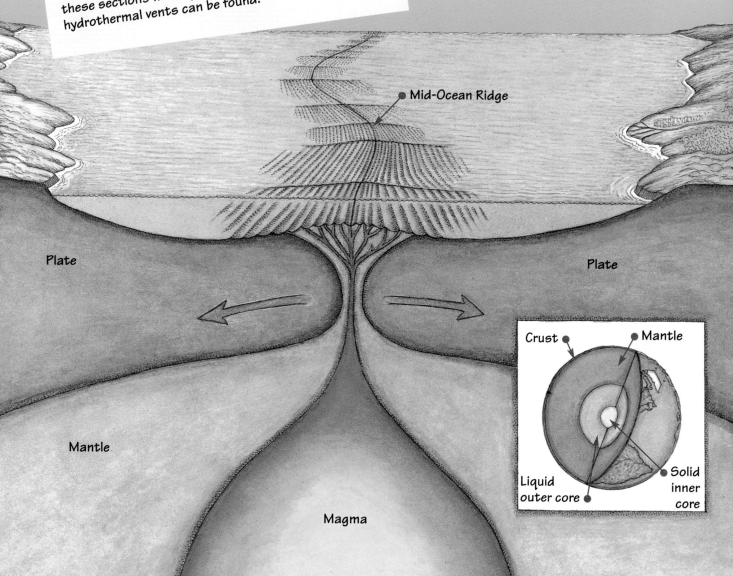

Mid-Ocean Ridge

Plate

Plate

Mantle

Magma

Crust

Mantle

Liquid outer core

Solid inner core

The Galápagos Rift is only one of many vent sites that have been studied. Scientists all over the world have collaborated to gather information on the locations of other possible vent sites.

could be found there. First, underwater equipment, such as cameras, was used to search for vents. Towed over the seafloor at the ends of steel cables, the cameras took pictures of the seafloor. Each picture recorded the location, time, and water temperature at the exact time the photograph was taken.

Temperatures in the deep ocean hardly vary from 2°C (35.6°F). If there is a change, it's very small, only a fraction of a degree. If the equipment recorded an increase in temperature, a vent might be nearby. This site would be a good place to dive. Working around the clock, the cameras sent back pictures of deep-sea mud and rocks, most with normal temperature readings. But thirteen pictures taken in the middle of the night showed a heap of white objects on the seafloor. These strange objects were clamshells. And at that exact spot, the water was also slightly warmer. The scientists didn't know why

This is *Alvin,* exploring a lava area on the seafloor. *Alvin's* lights illuminate only a small area around the submersible. Beyond this area the water is completely black.

The scientists didn't know how to explain the clamshells in the pictures. Some thought they might have been tossed overboard after an ocean clambake.

Deep-sea spider crabs live near vents as well as at other places on the seafloor.

the clamshells were there, but they had a name for their dive site. They called it "Clambake."

The following day, pilot Jack Donnelly from Woods Hole Oceanographic Institution (or WHOI, pronounced "HOO-ee"), a research institution located in Woods Hole, Massachusetts, and geologists Tjeerd van Andel and John Corliss of Oregon State University set out on the first dive. One and one-half hours later, *Alvin* was 2,400 meters (8,000 feet) deep, moving over black lava. The water temperature was 2°C (35.6°F). Outside the viewports, there was nothing to see but round, black rocks.

Then, *Alvin*'s heat-sensing probe began to beep. Everyone in the submersible got ready for action. They expected to find water a few thousandths of a degree warmer than normal, to collect a few rock and water samples, and then to return to the ship. But the probe continued to beep. *Alvin* was moving into water that was warmer…and warmer…and warmer.

Suddenly the view from *Alvin* changed. There were animals in every direction. Huge, white clams—some 25 centimeters (about 10 inches) across—big, brown mussels, and white crabs were everywhere. The divers saw an anemone, white tangles of what looked like cooked spaghetti draped over the rocks, and a peach-colored, fluffy ball that looked like a dandelion.

Scientists had always thought that there were almost no animals at such extreme depths. It was believed that very few animals could live so far from food produced at the ocean's sunlit surface. What were these animals? What were they doing here? How did they survive?

The scientists in *Alvin* that day knew that the animals they were seeing were unusual, but they were there to investigate the rocks. Turning their attention away from the animals, they saw rocks streaked with red and orange, colors that could have come from minerals mixed in the fluid that poured from the vents.

This was what the scientists had been hoping to find. Working quickly, they grabbed a few samples— some colored rocks and some mussels. Then, it was time

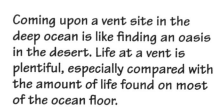

Coming upon a vent site in the deep ocean is like finding an oasis in the desert. Life at a vent is plentiful, especially compared with the amount of life found on most of the ocean floor.

The red numbers on the side of this picture are in every still photograph taken by *Alvin's* cameras. These numbers help identify each picture.

This is a tripod fish, named for its habit of resting on its fins. This type of fish is common in the deep sea.

These are spider crabs feasting on one of the big clams that can be found at some vents.

to go back the way they had come, rising through water that was black, then gray, and then blue, until they reached the surface.

What had they found? They weren't sure. But they knew where the answers were—straight down. So they dove again and again. On one dive, John Corliss was exploring Clambake with John Edmond, a geochemist from the Massachusetts Institute of Technology. They looked out *Alvin*'s tiny viewports and saw that the water in one place shimmered, the way the air sometimes does over a hot sidewalk. *Alvin*'s temperature gauge shot up to 8°C (46.4°F), an incredible reading in the deep sea. Could they have found a vent? They quickly took samples of the water and returned to the surface.

Back on the ship, everyone gathered around as a sample container was opened. A horrible smell filled the air—like the smell from a carton of rotten eggs dropped on the floor. The awful stink nearly drove everyone to the

This vent site is full of clams. Tightly closed clamshells house live clams. Open shells no longer hold clams. Those clams may have been eaten by other animals.

This is a deep-sea cucumber, a relative of the starfish. Some kinds of sea cucumbers can swim.

Feather-duster worms curl over the rocks. They live inside tubes.

Alvin's temperature probe can enter cracks in the rocky seafloor.

deck to breathe fresh sea air. The chemists aboard knew that smell. It was hydrogen sulfide, a gas that is poisonous to most animals.

Seawater is made of nearly the same things everywhere, and it doesn't contain hydrogen sulfide. Because volcanic activity often produces hydrogen sulfide, scientists expect to find it near active volcanoes or hot springs. But now geologists had found it in seawater at a vent site. The scientists believed there had to be a connection between the hydrogen sulfide and the volcanic rock on the seafloor. But what was the connection? The scientists had a puzzle piece, and now they had to fit it into place.

After that, new pieces of the discovery puzzle waited at every dive site. Divers found more and more vents. They saw lava stacks, or pillars, lava flows hardened into

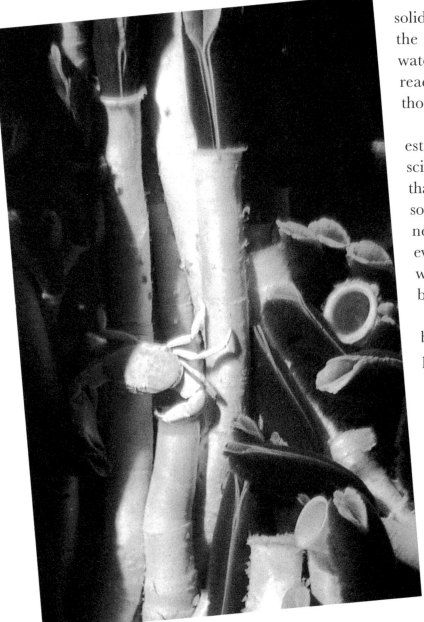

These are *Riftia*, giant tubeworms that live in large numbers at some Pacific Ocean vent sites. The small vent crab is probably looking for food.

solid rivers, and even a solid lava lake the size of a football field. And the water became warmer and warmer, reaching temperatures no one had thought possible.

But the strangest and most interesting things were the animals. The scientists returned with giant worms that lived in tubes longer than a person's arm and clams the size of dinner plates. No one on the ship had ever seen anything like them. What were they? The scientists radioed biologists they knew for advice.

Holger Jannasch, a WHOI biologist, was one of the first people to receive a call from the Galápagos group. "When I was called up here by Corliss…oh, I didn't believe it!" he remembered thinking. "I told him there are no such things on the seafloor!" He and other biologists urged the geologists to "collect everything!" The scientists tried. After 24 dives, scientists on *Alvin* had collected 100 rock samples, 88 water samples, more than 200 samples of animals and shells, and 20,000 photographs.

Preserving the animals was not easy. No one had thought they would need containers for anything other than rocks and seawater. Plastic containers and even plastic wrap from the ship's kitchen were used to wrap the huge worms and to make bags for other animals.

The scientists' resourcefulness paid off. On returning

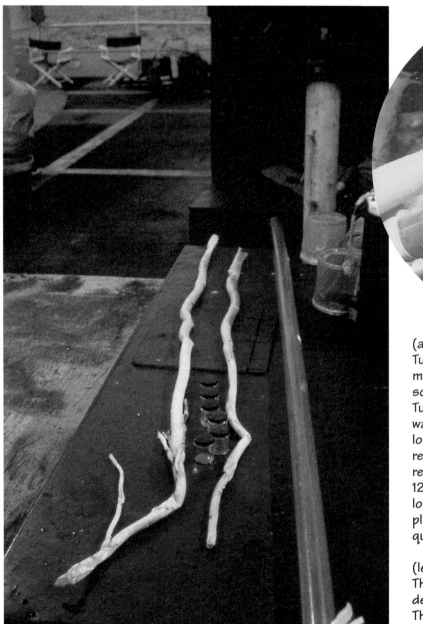

(above)
Tubeworms were one of the most spectacular new animals scientists found at the vents. Tubeworms live in clusters near warm vent water, sometimes looking like towering gardens of red-topped vines. A tubeworm's red top, or plume, is about 12 centimeters (about 5 inches) long. A tubeworm can extend its plume out of its tube and then quickly pull its plume inside.

(left)
The long, tan "ropes" lying on the deck here are actually tubeworms. The tubeworm on the left is almost two meters (about six feet) long.

to shore, they found that not only was the existence of communities of animals at such extreme depths a new discovery, but almost all the life forms they had found were totally unknown.

News of the find excited ocean scientists everywhere. Here was a whole new world to explore, a place unlike

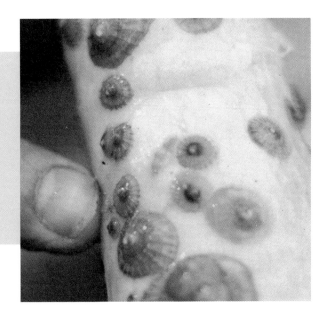

Do you ever find yourself looking for one thing, only to find something else? Sometimes the same thing happens to scientists. Learning more about geology was the reason for going to hydrothermal vents. Vent animals, like these deep-sea limpets attached to tubeworms, were an accidental discovery.

Some accidental discoveries are very mysterious. For example, the "Chinese checkerboard" creature (above), a living fossil with the scientific name *Paleodictyon nodosum*, was found near a hydrothermal vent in the Atlantic Ocean. When it was first seen in a photograph, it looked so strange to scientists that they thought their camera was broken. Very little is known about this "checkerboard," except that it is similar to creatures that lived hundreds of millions of years ago.

any on Earth. Holger Jannasch called it "one of the major biological discoveries of the twentieth century."

"Discovery" is a big word, but science moves in small steps. Scientists look at the pieces of a giant puzzle and fit them together, one by one. Since that first dive in 1977, scientists from all over the world have been working to solve the mysteries of hydrothermal vents and vent ecosystems. An ecosystem is living and nonliving things functioning together in an environment. To understand these ecosystems, scientists must first answer some questions.

Dudley Foster, who has piloted scientists to vent sites hundreds of times in *Alvin*, once said, "Aside from the first startling impact, science sees this forest and then [scientists] spend the next fifteen years looking at the trees.... What makes this forest? You have to look at the trees to figure out what the forest is made of."

This is a frame used for scale. It helps scientists determine the size of objects they are photographing and videotaping.

This is a camera system that records twenty seconds of video every day.

These tube-worms are very important inhabitants of the vent community.

This is where a crack in the seafloor allowed warm vent fluid to seep up.

This is part of *Alvin's* camera and photographic equipment.

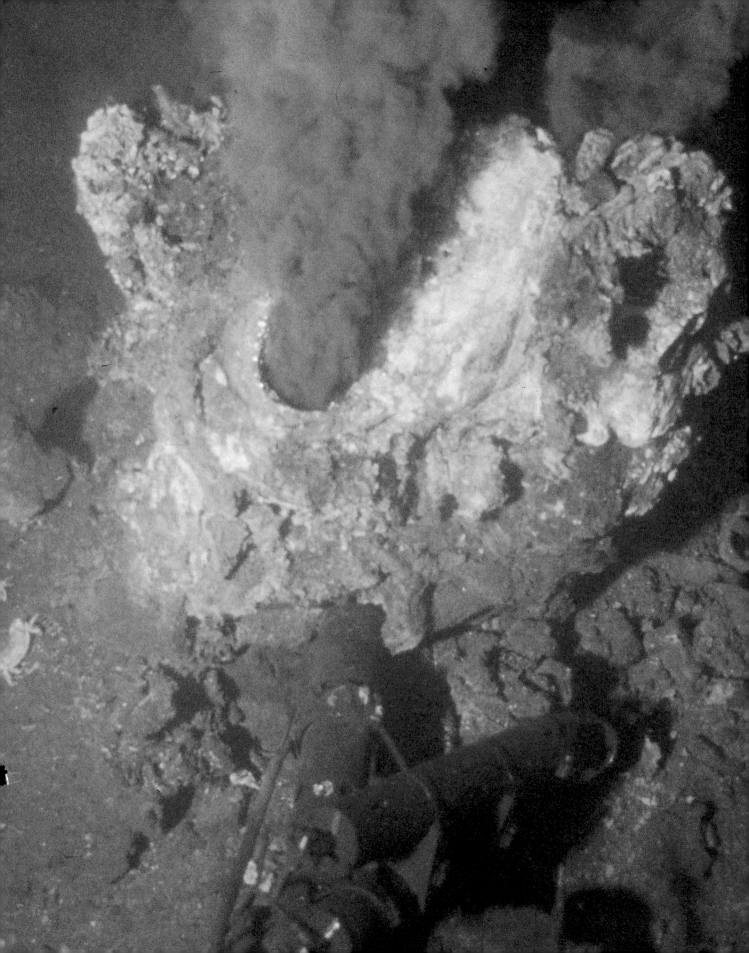

2

WHAT IS A HYDROTHERMAL VENT?

"[Vents are] ... incredibly beautiful. It's like going to one of the seven wonders of the world. It is a natural physical environment that is beyond your wildest dreams."—Geologist Dan Fornari

On a dive to a vent site off the coast of Mexico in 1979, scientists continued to explore the Mid-Ocean Ridge system. *Alvin's* pilot, Dudley Foster, and geologists saw what no person had seen before—a tall, thin, chimney-like stack topped by black clouds. Dudley later said that it looked like a locomotive blasting out smoke.

They knew it wasn't smoke because there was no air. It was a cloud of fluid shooting up from a hydrothermal vent. Why was it black? How hot was it? Could they get a sample? Dudley carefully inched *Alvin* closer to measure the fluid's temperature. He tried twice, getting a reading nobody could believe—73°C (163.4°F). Then, he gave up. He thought there was something wrong with the equipment. Only after the dive did the scientists see that the fluid had melted their temperature probe. The temperature had been above 180°C (356°F), hot enough to melt plastic—and *Alvin's* viewport if Dudley had moved closer. They had found the first black smoker vent.

How does a smoker form? Hydrothermal vents work a lot like hot springs and geysers, such as Old Faithful at Yellowstone Park. Geysers happen when water under the ground meets rock that's been heated by volcanic activity. In places such as Yellowstone, this rock is near the earth's surface and also near underground water.

(above)
This photo shows what happened when Alvin moved too close to a black smoker vent. It returned with patches of what looked like soot on its side!

(left)
You can see hot, poisonous clouds billow up through the opening of a black smoker.

19

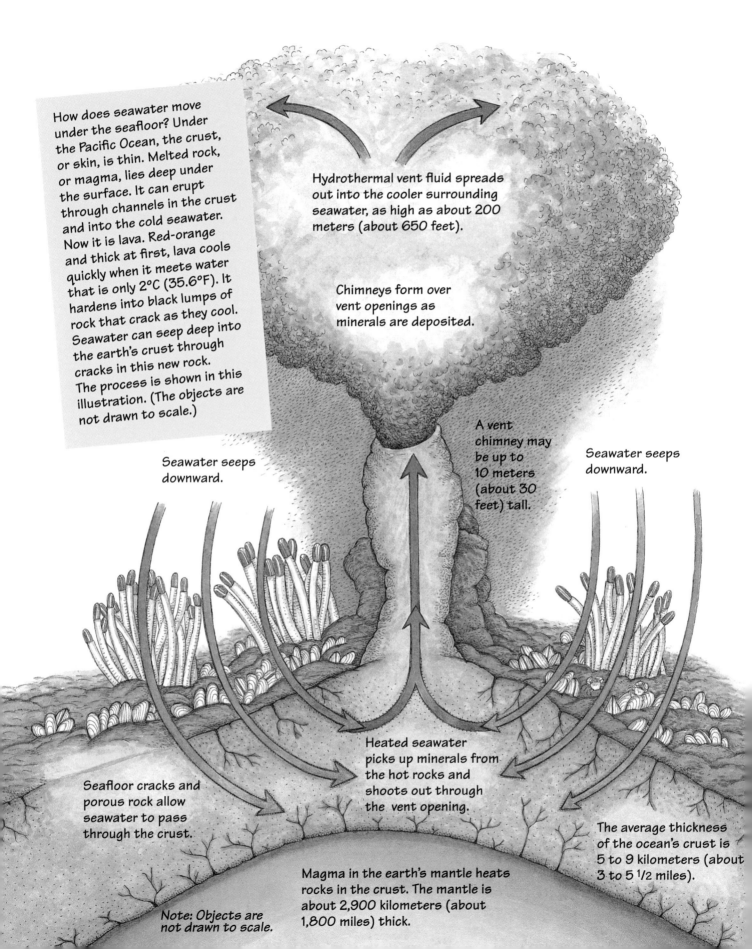

How does seawater move under the seafloor? Under the Pacific Ocean, the crust, or skin, is thin. Melted rock, or magma, lies deep under the surface. It can erupt through channels in the crust and into the cold seawater. Now it is lava. Red-orange and thick at first, lava cools quickly when it meets water that is only 2°C (35.6°F). It hardens into black lumps of rock that crack as they cool. Seawater can seep deep into the earth's crust through cracks in this new rock. The process is shown in this illustration. (The objects are not drawn to scale.)

Hydrothermal vent fluid spreads out into the cooler surrounding seawater, as high as about 200 meters (about 650 feet).

Chimneys form over vent openings as minerals are deposited.

A vent chimney may be up to 10 meters (about 30 feet) tall.

Seawater seeps downward.

Seawater seeps downward.

Seafloor cracks and porous rock allow seawater to pass through the crust.

Heated seawater picks up minerals from the hot rocks and shoots out through the vent opening.

The average thickness of the ocean's crust is 5 to 9 kilometers (about 3 to 5 1/2 miles).

Magma in the earth's mantle heats rocks in the crust. The mantle is about 2,900 kilometers (about 1,800 miles) thick.

Note: Objects are not drawn to scale.

Some lava hardens into pillow shapes like these.

The water becomes very hot and dissolves some of the minerals in the rocks. When the water is hot enough, steam forms, pressure builds, and a jet of water called a geyser shoots up to the surface and into the air.

Under the ocean, seawater seeps far down into the crust of the earth, just as rainwater seeps into land.

Other lava hardens into long rivers or sheets like these, or it piles up to form columns.

When the seawater meets hot rock, the water is heated and chemical reactions occur. Superhot seawater dissolves large amounts of minerals before it returns through cracks in the seafloor. A jet of hot fluid shoots up and out of a vent, meets cold seawater, and changes. The fluid's temperature drops rapidly, especially at the edges of the jet. This rapid cooling makes a sharp line between very hot and very cold water. When

(above)
The light-colored fluid from a white smoker vent comes out more slowly than the fluid from a black smoker. Some mineral deposits form tower-like shapes like these.

(below)
Shimmering water, or warm, rising vent fluid, can be seen in the center of this photograph.

vent fluid meets cold seawater, some of the minerals in the fluid become solid and fall from the vent fluid in tiny pieces. At a black smoker, these pieces are black, making the fluid look like black smoke. As solid particles form and fall in a process called precipitation, a crumbly chimney of mineral deposits builds. The minerals sometimes take fantastic shapes that look like towers and turrets on a castle, or even onions, sometimes two or three meters (about seven to ten feet) tall.

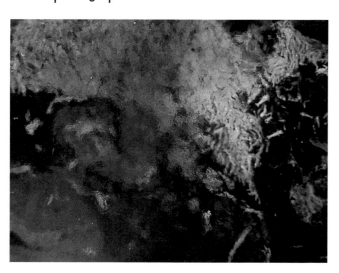

Black isn't the only color of vent fluid. Some hydrothermal vents pour out white or clear fluid. The fluid's color depends on its temperature and the kinds and amounts of minerals in it. Fluids find their way to vent openings from far below the seafloor. The path can be short and direct, allowing extremely hot (400°C or 752°F) fluid to escape. If the path is longer and cold seawater mixes into the fluid along the way, the fluid cools before it exits. Some fluid contains minerals that form white solid particles. They settle, or fall, from the fluid, forming white clouds around these vents, which are called white smokers.

Where warm fluid mixes with the cold seawater, the water seems to shimmer. "Shimmering water" is the coolest vent fluid. It flows more slowly than smoker jets. It still has a lot of minerals in it, but not enough to form solid particles.

Far above the vent opening, hot vent fluid mixed with seawater is buoyant because higher temperatures decrease water's density. The less-dense water is lighter, and it forms a plume, or cloud, that rises into the ocean. Plumes can rise 200 meters (about 650 feet) above the seafloor and spread 100 kilometers (about 60 miles) wide.

The geologists who discovered vents expected to find warm water, but not water that was *hot*. They also found that vent fluid contained minerals and chemicals, including hydrogen sulfide. Might all these chemicals gushing out of vents affect seawater's composition everywhere?

This question interests another kind of scientist—a geochemist. Ocean geochemists study the chemicals and chemical reactions in seawater and in the rocks and soil beneath the water. Geochemists want to know why seawater is salty and why it stays salty even though all the world's rivers pour freshwater into it. Perhaps chemicals from vents help keep seawater salty. Before they can be sure, scientists need to know how many vents there are, where they are, and how much fluid flows from them.

A vent doesn't last forever. Vents can stop flowing because crust shifts or because a chimney falls over. They may even stop flowing because minerals or animals cover and clog the vent opening, shutting it off. The area in this photograph is an inactive, or dead, vent site at the Atlantic Mid-Ocean Ridge. Each of the towers was once a vent. A new vent may soon form nearby, or the area may remain inactive for years. As of yet, there's no way to know.

(above)
The Tubeworm Barbecue site was home to a large animal community in 1989. The animals were killed by a lava flow in 1991.

(below)
Predicting potential vent sites requires a lot of information and work. Here, scientists Dan Fornari and Susan Humphris analyze vent data.

Geologist Dan Fornari is one scientist trying to answer these questions. He studies the structure of undersea volcanic areas, maps them, and then tries to predict where volcanic activity and vent sites will occur. It is a long and painstaking job that involves many people and lasts many years. Dan works with geologists from all over the globe. They are working together to assemble pieces of the vent puzzle.

Scientists' findings are usually the result of careful planning and work, but sometimes they're lucky. In 1991 Dan, along with geologist Rachel Haymon, dove to a site in the Pacific that they had studied for ten years and knew well. This site had been home to a large number of vent animals. This time, something was different—the animals were gone. A lava flow had just occurred, maybe only hours before the scientists arrived. "We now knew what a brand-new lava flow looked like," Dan said.

They also had the chance to watch a new vent community from its beginning. Dan and others went back to "Tubeworm Barbecue" (named for the effect of the lava on the tubeworms) five times over the next seven years, taking photographs of the animals that returned to the site. Tubeworm Barbecue isn't the only vent site being studied so closely. Deep-sea cameras have been placed at other vents around the world, taking pictures for several months. Scientists use the photographs and information they collect about the chemistry, physics, and biology of the vent sites to learn how vents change over time. Everything they learn adds more pieces to the big puzzle.

Meg Tivey (right), a WHOI geochemist, studies chimney samples like these to understand how different minerals form chimneys and mounds. Mounds are rounded shapes that vent deposits sometimes make. Meg found that minerals can be deposited in separate rings around chimneys and mounds. Rings of zinc, copper, and even silver or gold can sometimes be found around a hydrothermal vent. The pattern of mineral rings found at vents helps geologists identify mineral deposits in volcanic areas on land as well.

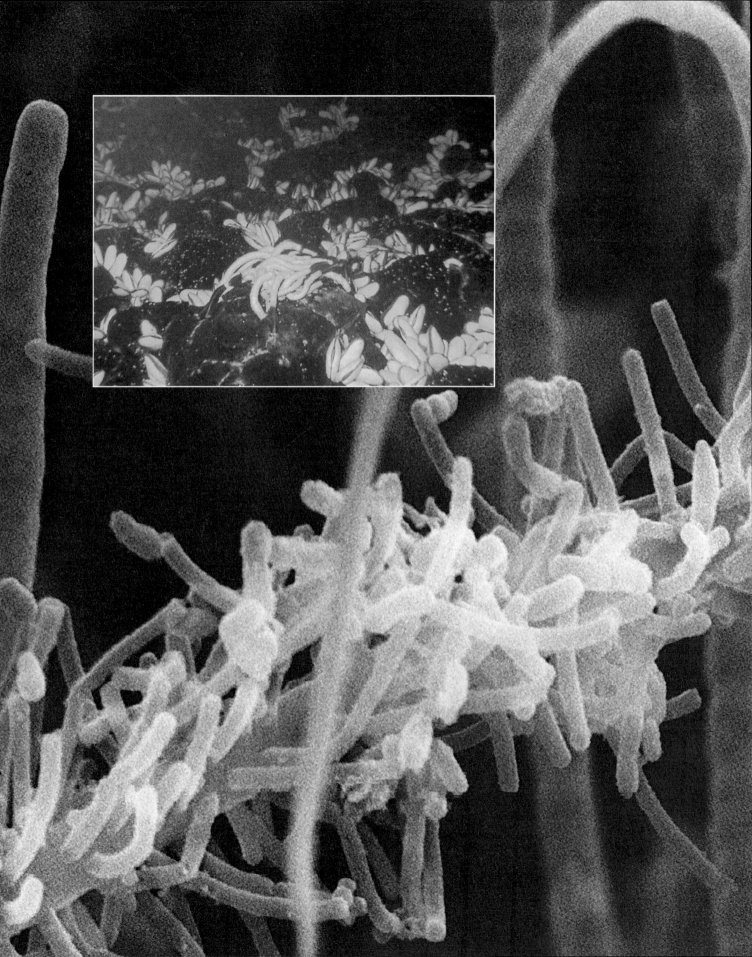

3

BACTERIAL BEGINNINGS

"[Bacteria] can survive almost anything. And we don't know whether resting bacteria can survive a hundred years, or thousands, or millions. They are there. They are just there, waiting. And when they grow, they grow in large numbers."—Biologist Holger Jannasch

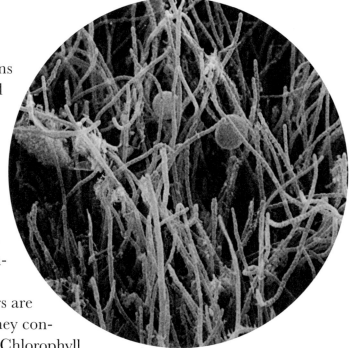

Once a vent has formed and fluid begins to flow, life can grow there. And it all depends on bacteria. Bacteria are very small cells. They are everywhere, in water, on land, on all living things, and also in the deep sea. Food in most of the deep sea is scarce. But some bacteria can solve that problem. These bacteria are primary producers, living things that make their own food instead of consuming other living things.

On land, almost all primary producers are green plants. Plants are green because they contain a green chemical called chlorophyll. Chlorophyll absorbs energy from sunlight. Plants use this energy to combine carbon dioxide from the air with hydrogen from water to make carbohydrates, releasing oxygen at the same time. This process, called photosynthesis, is the basis of most life on Earth. Plants use carbohydrates for their own energy, life, and growth. Animals get carbohydrates by eating plants. Animals also breathe oxygen that plants release during photosynthesis.

In the ocean, almost all primary producers are tiny, one-celled plants called phytoplankton. Phytoplankton,

(above)
The vent bacteria in this photograph are magnified 500 times. They use hydrogen sulfide as an energy source and can be, in turn, a food source for other organisms.

(left)
A similar kind of bacteria, magnified 5,000 times in this photograph, is found along the rims of white vent clams (inset).

27

sometimes called the "grass of the sea," need sunlight for photosynthesis. Because sunlight doesn't reach much deeper than about 120 meters (about 400 feet), phytoplankton live in the upper part of the ocean.

Most animals in the ocean depend on phytoplankton for food, either directly or indirectly. They may eat phytoplankton, animals that eat phytoplankton, or other animals. Even in the deep ocean, most animals eat small bits of plant and animal matter that settle to the seafloor from the surface. This means that they, too, depend on phytoplankton, photosynthesis, and sunlight for food.

Like plants on land and phytoplankton in the ocean, some deep-sea bacteria make carbohydrates from carbon dioxide and water. But these bacteria use the chemicals

Have you ever smelled a marsh at low tide? If you have, then you probably remember the smell of rotten eggs. But what you're really smelling is chemosynthesis at work. Some bacteria in seawater use chemicals instead of sunlight to grow. They are called chemosynthetic bacteria. These bacteria can also live in places, like salt marshes, that contain chemicals such as hydrogen sulfide and oxygen. Here, researchers take water samples from a marsh.

Energy Movers

Primary producers use a source of energy to produce food from simple molecules in the environment. Primary producers are at the bottom of food chains. A food chain is a way to show the transfer of energy from producers to consumers. Animals, fungi, and most bacteria are consumers, and they are higher up on food chains. Their energy comes as they consume the matter in plants or animals.

The process is called photosynthesis when primary producers use sunlight as their energy source. It is called chemosynthesis when they use a chemical, such as hydrogen sulfide, as their energy source.

The food chain on the left depends on photosynthesis. The chlorophyll in plants absorbs light, and plants use the light as energy to make food. The plants' energy is then transferred to animals, such as rabbits, that eat the plants.

The food chain on the right depends on chemosynthesis. Certain bacteria use the energy from hydrogen sulfide from hydrothermal vents to produce food. The bacteria's energy is transferred to the limpets as they eat the bacteria.

Animals
(rabbits)

Plants

Sunlight

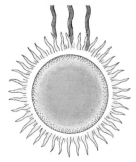

Sun

Photosynthesis

Animals
(limpets)

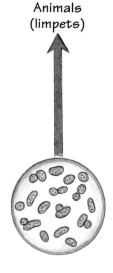

Bacteria

Hydrogen
sulfide

Hydrothermal vent

Chemosynthesis

Patches of light-colored chemosynthetic bacteria grow in visible mats at certain vents.

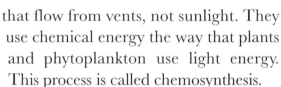

This image shows a close-up view, magnified 3,700 times, of several kinds of bacteria growing on a sulfur-containing deposit at a vent. Many of these bacteria may be chemosynthetic.

that flow from vents, not sunlight. They use chemical energy the way that plants and phytoplankton use light energy. This process is called chemosynthesis.

The chemical that bacteria living at hydrothermal vents use most for chemosynthesis is hydrogen sulfide. Though hydrogen sulfide is poisonous to us and to most living things, it's not poisonous to these bacteria. When hydrogen sulfide is present, the bacteria begin to grow and form the basis of life at hydrothermal vents. Holger Jannasch was a microbiologist, a scientist who studies microscopic organisms, especially bacteria. He said, "If these bacteria that do this chemosynthesis weren't there, there would be no [vent] animals in the deep sea. They just couldn't grow there—there would be no food.…Bacteria fill the role of green plants in an environment without light.…It seems microbes [bacteria] can do anything."

Alvin's Accidental Discovery

The research submersible *Alvin* hasn't always had smooth sailing. In 1968 just as a pilot and two scientists were getting in for a dive, a broken cable caused the submersible to sink about 1,500 meters (about 5,000 feet). The submersible was recovered (inset) ten months later—with a lunch that had been left aboard. Apples, bologna sandwiches, and a thermos of broth had spent nearly a year in the deep sea. Yet when found, they were nearly as fresh as the day they were lost.

Bacteria specialists Holger Jannasch and Carl Wirsen looked at (and even tasted and smelled) the lost lunch. They began to think about bacteria living at deep-sea pressures. Working with engineers and other scientists, they developed devices to bring up bacteria for study.

They found that bacteria grow much more slowly, and that plant and animal matter decomposes, or rots, much more slowly in the deep sea than they do at sea level. This may mean that garbage put into the sea each year doesn't decompose. What Jannasch called "*Alvin's* involuntary experiment" began his interest in deep-sea bacteria.

But how do bacteria live before a new vent forms? WHOI microbiologist Carl Wirsen found that the bacteria can also live off sulfur chemicals found in the volcanic rocks on the seafloor. These chemicals make it possible for the bacteria to survive, so they are already present before a vent forms. The rocks near where vents form are porous, or full of tiny holes, and the bacteria live in and around these holes. When vents form, warm vent fluid seeps through the holes in the rocks, providing bacteria with an almost unlimited energy source. After a

Scientists dive again and again to hydrothermal vent sites to find answers to questions they have—and to find more questions. Carl Wirsen, seen entering Alvin above, has dived to the ocean floor many times to study bacteria.

vent begins, it doesn't take long for them to grow. In a short time, mats of bacteria blanket the rocks. "If you take up any surface," said Jannasch, "the surface of a tube, or lava rocks, or deposits, or the surface of a clam, they have a thick film of bacteria on them."

Bacteria are also in the water. In 1991 when an eruption covered the Tubeworm Barbecue site with lava, scientists reported seeing so much bacteria blowing out from a vent that they named the vent "Snowblower." Carl Wirsen and another WHOI microbiologist, Craig Taylor, study the bacteria at Snowblower. They have found that the bacteria grow in the cracks and channels of rocks near warm hydrothermal vents. A change in water flow can flush the bacteria into the seawater.

Another strange kind of microorganism that lives near vents is archaea [ar-KEE-ah]. Because archaea grow in temperatures at or above 100°C (212°F), they are called thermophiles, or "heat lovers." Known to live in hot springs on land, archaea were also found inside the walls of smoker chimneys and in the hot vent fluid under the seafloor, where there is no oxygen. They survive in temperatures once thought too high for life to exist—temperatures as high as 113°C (235°F).

The steady supply of chemicals from a vent allows bacteria to grow abundantly. In turn, they support life at a vent. They are the primary producers of a vent community, providing food for some very strange animals.

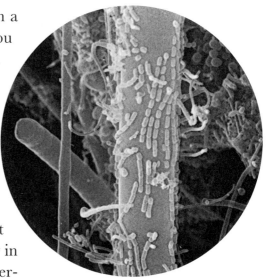

Bacteria come in many shapes and sizes. In this image, magnified 2,000 times, small bacteria are growing on much larger bacteria.

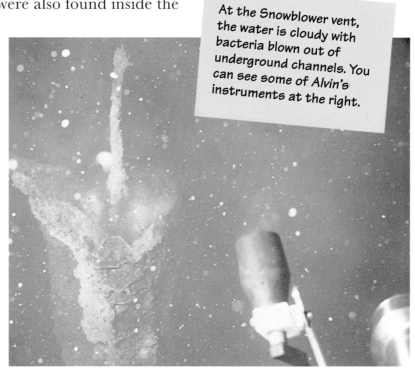

At the Snowblower vent, the water is cloudy with bacteria blown out of underground channels. You can see some of Alvin's instruments at the right.

4

WHO'S HERE?

"The crabs fight with each other over prey and are the clowns of the system—they check out, yank on, [and] fiddle with anything they find."—Biologist Lauren Mullineaux

Before long, animals arrive at vents to eat the growing population of bacteria. But what animals come? Most of the animals that live at hydrothermal vents live nowhere else in the ocean. With all the food there, why don't other deep-sea animals come? Part of the answer is that most animals can't survive in or near hydrothermal vents. Vent animals have differences that make them perfect for their environment. They are able to live near and eat matter that poisons most animals, and they can survive temperatures too warm for other deep-sea creatures.

(above)
The Pompeii worm lives in hard tubes on the walls of the hottest smoker vents.

(left)
Ruth Turner, a biologist at Harvard University, holds a tubeworm brought to the surface on one of the first trips to the Galápagos vents. At first scientists didn't know how tubeworms survived.

To study animals, scientists first classify, or group, them. Ecologists, or biologists who study the way organisms interact with their environments, often classify animals according to what and how they eat. Among vent animals there are grazers, suspension feeders, predators, scavengers, and a few odd animals that don't fit easily into any group.

Grazers eat the soft layers of bacteria on rocks and on the shells and tubes of other animals. Snails, crabs, and limpets are some of the grazers at vents.

Big, brown mussels are found at many vents. One kind is called *Bathymodiolus thermophilus.* The first part of their name means "deep mussel," and the second part of their name means "heat lover." Mussels have bacteria living inside them, but they also can feed by straining food bits out of the water.

Ghostly white crabs crawl all over the vent, eating just about anything. They even pinch off parts of unwary tubeworms.

Suspension feeders remove tiny bits of food, including clumps of bacteria, from the water. Some strain food out of the water, and others let bits of food settle on sticky parts of their bodies. Then, they eat whatever sticks. Suspension feeders at vents include mussels, barnacles, and feather-duster worms.

Predators, or animals that eat other animals, also live at vents. One kind, the anemone, has a stalklike body and tentacles like petals. Anemones use their tentacles to capture small animals that swim by. Sometimes there are so many anemones that they nearly form rings around vent chimneys. Scavengers, such as white crabs and brittle stars, relatives of the starfish, are common at vents. They feed on live or dead animals, or bacteria, eating whatever they can catch or find.

Flowerlike anemones live at many vents. Found alone on a rocky chimney or by the hundreds in thick beds, they can be purple, pink, or white, living in what look like carefully tended gardens. Being predators, anemones trap small animals swimming through the water.

Tubeworms and clams don't fit into any of these categories.

Vent sites may be hundreds or thousands of kilometers apart. How do all of these unusual animals find their homes? Lauren Mullineaux, a biologist at WHOI, has been trying to answer this particular question. Most adult vent animals are attached to rocks. But even those animals that are free to move would have difficulty reaching vents hundreds of kilometers away. When vent fluids stop flowing, the adult animals that live there die. Scientists have found that some vents last only a short time—maybe as little as ten years.

At some vents long, white worms drape in tangles over lava rocks. Scientists nicknamed them "spaghetti worms." It was discovered later that this kind of worm also lives in mud in shallow water.

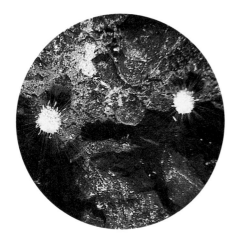

These golf-ball-sized, peach-colored "dandelions" are actually colonies of animals called siphonophores. Each colony is a cluster of small, saclike individuals living together and feeding on smaller animals. The whole cluster is anchored to rocks with long tentacles. Otherwise, the siphonophores would drift away like dandelions gone to seed. They are very delicate. None of this species has ever been brought to the surface alive.

So how do animals reach another vent? The answer involves the larval, or baby, animals. Most vent animals live the first part of their lives as small, swimming larvae. When they settle at vent sites, they change into their adult forms.

Larvae of vent animals have been found in the buoyant plumes that rise above vents. Scientists think the larvae ride the plumes like people ride an elevator, moving upward as high as 200 meters (about 660 feet). The plumes also carry them many kilometers away from the vent. Scientists think the currents may carry the larvae to new vents. After all, spider babies travel on the wind. Why can't deep-sea babies travel on the currents? But a harder question remains. How do larvae know when to leave the current? Do they sense a certain kind of rock? Or do they sense a particular smell in the water?

One way biologists like Lauren have tried to answer these kinds of questions is by placing flat pieces of rock or glass on the seafloor, then returning later to see what animals have attached themselves to the rock or glass.

These feather-duster worms, which live in tubes they build and attach to the rocks, are similar to worms that live in shallow water. They spread a crown of feathery tentacles in the water to catch tiny bits of plant and animal matter.

Do You See What I See?

Cindy Van Dover is a deep-sea ecologist, a scientist who studies the connections among plants and animals and their deep ocean environment. One new animal she studied was a shrimp that was found swarming by the thousands at some vents in the Atlantic (below right). "I couldn't help but notice a pair of bright, reflective spots on the back of the shrimp," she said. Could they be eyes of some kind? Tests found that the spots contained some of the same material found in many animals' eyes. She was right. The shrimp have a kind of eyes. But what would they look at in the dark?

Cindy began to think—maybe there is light at vents that we can't see. She went to sea with a digital camera (right) able to record light levels too low for a human eye to see. "Alvin was lifted off the deck carrying the camera," she recalls. Cindy was not along on the dive and waited all day for a message from someone in the submersible.

"At the end of the dive, with the submersible well into its hour-long ascent, I gave up on learning anything about the success of the experiment and left the room. On returning, I was handed a note—a message from the submersible with only two words: 'vents glow.'"

shrimp

This experiment works in shallow water, but it's more difficult to do in the deep water where vents are found. But Lauren has come up with an approach. She uses *Alvin* to place large pieces of volcanic rock called basalt near vents on the seafloor. Returning one year later, Lauren finds young vent animals settled and growing on the basalt.

Lauren also tries to raise vent animals in her lab. She creates deep-sea temperature and pressure conditions so she can observe how vent animals grow and behave. So far, the larvae in the lab grow, but don't attach themselves and reach adulthood. Why this happens remains a mystery.

How Far Apart Are the Vents?

There's no one answer to this question. There isn't a way yet to know just where lava will flow or just where vent fluid will rise. Some vent sites are thousands of kilometers from each other, while others are strung in a line only meters apart like beads on a necklace.

Hydrothermal vents were first discovered in the Pacific Ocean, but there are also vents in the Atlantic Ocean, and probably in the Indian Ocean, the Arctic Ocean, and near Antarctica. The markers on the image below show the vent sites that have been discovered so far.

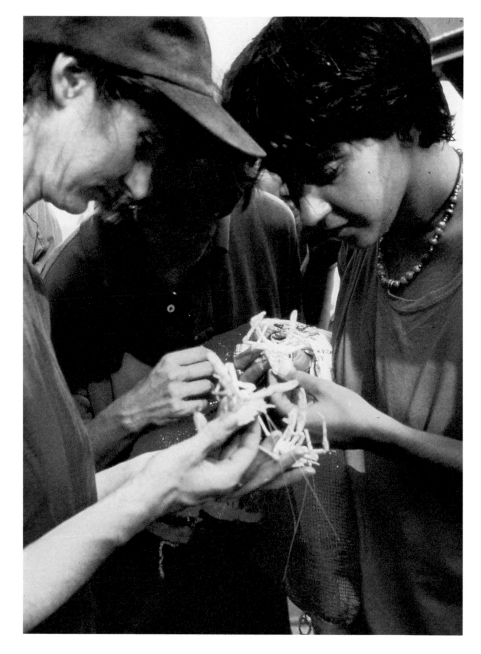

Lauren Mullineaux (left) and Anna Metaxis examine crabs brought up from a hydrothermal vent.

Ecologists ask if different animals live at different vents around the world. Stands of tubeworms, for example, live in the Pacific Ocean, but they have not been found in the Atlantic. Scientists also want to know if the same animals at different vents are related to each other. Mussels at one vent may look identical to mussels at

Holger Jannasch carefully holds one of the deep-sea spider crabs that are sometimes found near vents. They can grow to a large size, and their backs and legs are spiny.

another vent hundreds of kilometers away, but still be genetically different. Why do animals appear at one vent, but not another? Why do unrelated animals at different vents look so much alike? These are questions that scientists are working to answer.

In the past twenty years, scientists have learned a lot about vent animals. Keeping careful records of which species of animals are found at which vents gives scientists clues about where one animal's range, or area, ends and another animal's range begins. It also helps them know how far vent animals can travel. But almost nothing is known about vent animals' behavior because it is difficult to observe them in their environment and they seldom survive in labs. Even what some of the animals eat remains unknown. Some of the animals don't eat at all. There is still much to learn about these creatures.

Whale Fall!

Vent animals can sometimes be found in other places besides vents. The most surprising place is the remains of the bodies of great whales, which sink from the surface. Ordinarily food from the surface is eaten before it gets to the deep sea, but something as big as a whale reaches the bottom. The whale's bones provide food for bacteria, which produce hydrogen sulfide. This source of hydrogen sulfide lets vent animals settle there.

Scientists think that dead whales might provide "stepping-stones" for vent animals, places where drifting larvae can settle, grow, and produce larvae of their own that might reach a new vent.

5

COOPERATIVE LIVING

"You know, so much depends on...recognizing a discovery when you see it. If your mind's not prepared, you'll walk right by something."—Biologist Bob Hessler

Probably the most amazing vent animals of all are the tubeworms and the huge, white clams. They are the largest animals at Pacific Ocean vents. They arrive quickly, grow fast, and seem perfectly suited to their odd world.

One thing makes tubeworms and white clams different from most other vent animals. In fact, it makes them different from almost all animals. They have no usable mouths, stomachs, or intestines. They have no way to take in food at all. Ecologists can't classify them as grazers, suspension feeders, predators, or scavengers. So what are they?

Standing beside a hydrothermal vent, a tall, white tubeworm extends the red plume at the top of its body. Is it eating? Yes and no. Holger Jannasch said, "It has given up eating altogether." So how does it stay alive?

At first this question stumped biologists. An answer came to Colleen Cavanaugh, now a biologist at Harvard University, while she listened to a lecture on tubeworms. The speaker explained that white crystals made of sulfur had been found in tubeworms' bodies. Biologists knew that chemosynthetic bacteria that use hydrogen sulfide sometimes produce sulfur. They also knew that bacteria

(above and left)
Riftia pachyptila is the largest and most spectacular tubeworm. Its tubes are white, and the worm has a bright red plume. Why is it red? Because the plume is filled with the worm's blood, which contains hemoglobin, the same compound that makes our blood red. "When the hydrogen sulfide comes up in big plumes, it [takes the oxygen out of the water]," *said Holger Jannasch.* "If animals can't store oxygen, they die. They keep it in hemoglobin; hemoglobin's job is to store and transport oxygen.... It's a red compound, and therefore the [heads of the] worms are red; it makes sense."

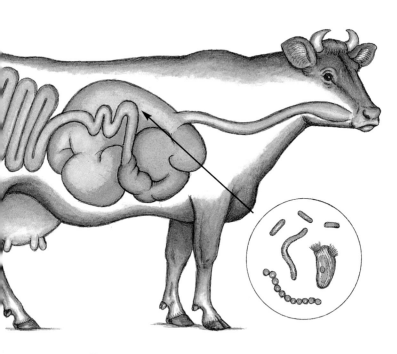

sometimes live inside animals' tissues. Colleen realized that bacteria could live inside tubeworms and could provide them with the nutrition they needed. Colleen jumped from her seat and announced her idea to the class.

Colleen spent years working to prove her theory. She carefully looked for bacteria inside a tubeworm. Eventually she found them, huge numbers of them in a special part of the worm's body. She was right. Tubeworms and bacteria are symbionts. This means they live together and keep each other alive in a special relationship called symbiosis. The tubeworm gives the bacteria a place to live and actually delivers the poisonous hydrogen sulfide the bacteria need.

How does this work? Researchers found that tubeworm blood contains hemoglobin, the same substance that gives our blood its red color. The hemoglobin picks up oxygen from seawater and carries it to the worm's tissues. But it also picks up hydrogen sulfide from vent fluid and delivers it, along with oxygen, to the bacteria living inside the tubeworm. Oxygen and hydrogen sulfide both enter the blood through the tubeworm's plume, which is bright red because it is filled with blood and hemoglobin.

Inside a tubeworm, bacteria use the hydrogen sulfide for energy and to produce carbohydrates. Some of the carbohydrates are used as food by the tubeworm. This way, both the bacteria and the tubeworm benefit from living together.

At first, biologists thought that the giant, white clams had neither mouths nor stomachs. Further investigation showed that they did, but they actually get their nutrition through a symbiotic relationship with bacteria, just as the

Partners

A partnership between two organisms in which both benefit is called symbiosis (from a Greek word that means "living together"). Some vent animals form symbiotic relationships with bacteria, but other examples of symbiosis occur on land.

Cows, for example, have symbiotic relationships with tiny microbes, or microscopic organisms. Cows eat grass, but they can't digest it. Why don't they starve? It's because they have partners. Cows have four stomachs, each with its own function. In the first stomach are microbes that help digest the grass a cow eats. It's a great partnership—the microbes have a home and a food supply, and the cow receives nutrition from the grass it eats.

worms do. But clams settle in cooler water farther from a vent. There's little hydrogen sulfide in the water around them. So how do they supply enough hydrogen sulfide for the bacteria living inside their tissues?

A clue came when scientists noticed that hydrogen sulfide spilled into the water when they picked up clams from the vent rocks. They learned that clams insert a part of their body called the foot into cracks in the rocks, plugging the cracks. Inside the cracks is vent fluid filled with hydrogen sulfide.

Big, brown mussels live at many vents, too. They settle at the same time tubeworms do, but they survive longer when vent fluid decreases. One explanation is that they have two ways to eat. They have bacteria inside their tissues, but they also have a mouth and digestive system. This means that if vent fluids begin to decrease, mussels can continue to live at the vent site. Even after vent fluids stop flowing, mussels can sometimes be found living at the site.

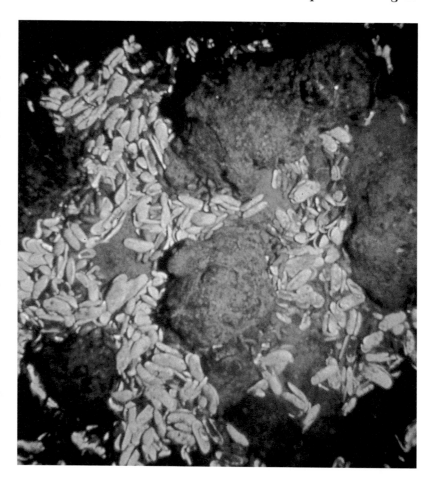

Calyptogena magnifica is the big, white clam seen in the first photographs of vents. They can grow to be ten inches long and are blood-red inside, unlike most clams. And also unlike normal clams, they don't eat food. They live off compounds that bacteria make inside their bodies.

The partnership between bacteria and vent animals is very important for the vent community. Tubeworms, clams, and the other symbiotic animals let bacteria live near the sulfide-rich vents instead of being carried away by currents. Scientists have found that these symbiotic bacteria grow much better than bacteria that live in the water nearby. They also found that animals that have

Pompeii worms actually build their tubes on smoker chimneys, where temperatures are very hot.

symbiotic bacteria have more food than other nearby animals. This explains why they grow so much larger than other vent animals. And they need to grow quickly. A vent may not last long. Animals are in a race to settle, grow, and reproduce before a vent stops flowing.

Some other animals at a vent have different ways to keep bacteria close. Two kinds of vent animals, a small shrimp that lives at Atlantic vent sites and the Pompeii [pom-PAY] worm that lives at Pacific vent sites, are covered with so much bacteria that they look furry. In both cases, scientists think that the bacterial "fur" may be more than accidental.

Colleen Cavanaugh, Cindy Van Dover, and Carl Wirsen have all been puzzled by what vent shrimp eat. They have seen shrimp swarm around vent openings at black smokers, darting in and out of the plumes. Carl and Cindy have each seen shrimp scooping up and eating bits of black sulfide from vent chimneys. They think the shrimp are eating bacteria that grow on the chimneys. The shrimp also seem to clean their shells off after eating, a normal shrimp behavior. But parts of their shells are hollow and full of chemosynthetic bacteria. Both Colleen and Carl think the shrimp may be "farming" the bacteria. They think the shrimp stay near the vent fluid to provide the hydrogen sulfide for their "crop" and then eat the bacteria that grow on them.

No one knows whether the heat-loving Pompeii worms are also cleaning off and eating their bacteria. Some scientists have suggested that the bacteria provide a protective coat, almost like a suit of armor, against the poisonous sulfides. If the bacteria absorb the hydrogen sulfide, then the sulfide isn't absorbed into the worm's body. It's another mystery for biologists to solve.

At Atlantic Ocean vent sites, shrimp gather in huge numbers on smoker chimneys. As Cindy Van Dover noted, "Every time you go there, it's shrimp, it's shrimp, it's shrimp."

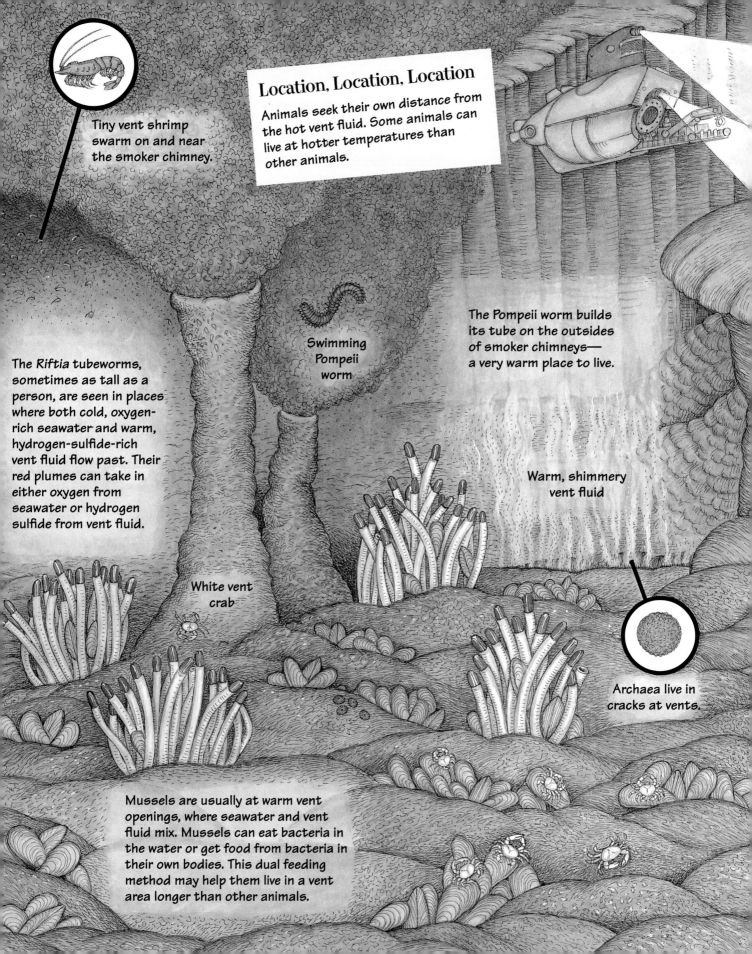

Tiny vent shrimp swarm on and near the smoker chimney.

Location, Location, Location

Animals seek their own distance from the hot vent fluid. Some animals can live at hotter temperatures than other animals.

Swimming Pompeii worm

The Pompeii worm builds its tube on the outsides of smoker chimneys— a very warm place to live.

The *Riftia* tubeworms, sometimes as tall as a person, are seen in places where both cold, oxygen-rich seawater and warm, hydrogen-sulfide-rich vent fluid flow past. Their red plumes can take in either oxygen from seawater or hydrogen sulfide from vent fluid.

Warm, shimmery vent fluid

White vent crab

Archaea live in cracks at vents.

Mussels are usually at warm vent openings, where seawater and vent fluid mix. Mussels can eat bacteria in the water or get food from bacteria in their own bodies. This dual feeding method may help them live in a vent area longer than other animals.

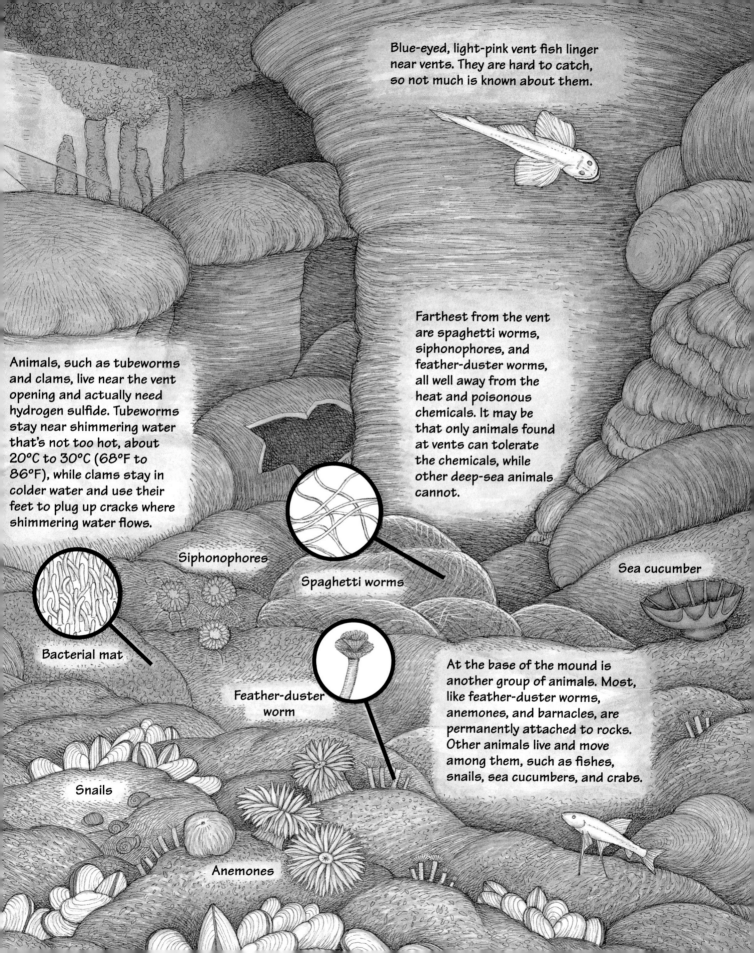

Blue-eyed, light-pink vent fish linger near vents. They are hard to catch, so not much is known about them.

Animals, such as tubeworms and clams, live near the vent opening and actually need hydrogen sulfide. Tubeworms stay near shimmering water that's not too hot, about 20°C to 30°C (68°F to 86°F), while clams stay in colder water and use their feet to plug up cracks where shimmering water flows.

Farthest from the vent are spaghetti worms, siphonophores, and feather-duster worms, all well away from the heat and poisonous chemicals. It may be that only animals found at vents can tolerate the chemicals, while other deep-sea animals cannot.

Siphonophores

Spaghetti worms

Sea cucumber

Bacterial mat

Feather-duster worm

At the base of the mound is another group of animals. Most, like feather-duster worms, anemones, and barnacles, are permanently attached to rocks. Other animals live and move among them, such as fishes, snails, sea cucumbers, and crabs.

Snails

Anemones

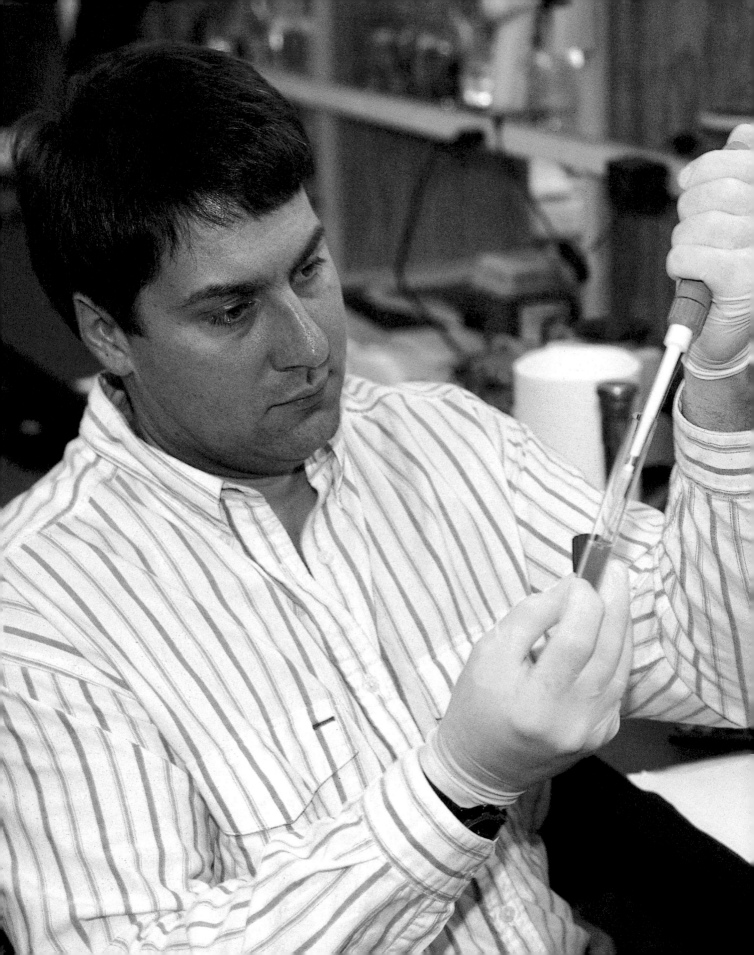

6
WHAT'S NEXT?

"Who are they? Where do they come from?"—Biologist Ken Halanych

The discovery of hydrothermal vents and their abundant animal communities came as a complete surprise. But after twenty years of work, scientists have learned a lot about the vents. While they continue to collect pieces of the puzzle, new researchers are joining the effort, often taking the work in different directions.

One big piece of the puzzle that remains unsolved is where vent animals come from and how they move from vent to vent. Raising vent larvae to adulthood, as Lauren Mullineaux is trying to do, will help answer that question.

WHOI biologist Ken Halanych wants to know how animals first began living at hydrothermal vents. How did they evolve? Did they once live in shallow water and then move to deep water? Have these animals existed for a long time? Ken asks, "Who are they? Where do they come from? How long have they been there? How much are they changing?" One way he tries to answer these questions is by studying the DNA, or the genetic code, of vent animals. He wants to know how closely related vent animals are to each other and to animals living in other places.

Vent research, however, now goes beyond the vents.

(above)
These two kinds of vent shrimp are found at sites in the Atlantic. Although they look very different, scientists have determined that they are the same species.

(left)
At work in the lab, scientist Ken Halanych prepares to analyze the DNA of vent animals to see how closely related they are.

People are finding ways to use what vent scientists are learning. Deep-ocean drilling, for example, has uncovered deposits of metal ores (minerals containing metals) beneath the vents. In the future, vents can serve as models for the way mineral deposits in volcanic areas form. This may lead to improved mining techniques on land.

Heat-loving archaea and bacteria from vents and hot springs produce compounds that have helped researchers make fast DNA analysis possible, take metals from ores and oil from some soils, and create high-temperature detergents for industrial cleaning processes. Molecular biologists, scientists who study the chemistry of cells, examine vent bacteria so that they might find compounds that can be used as new antibiotics or to help slow the growth of tumors.

Another idea is changing the way scientists study vents. Instead of scientists diving to the vent, the vent is going to the scientists. On a recent expedition to the North Pacific, four 2-meters-tall (about 7-feet-tall) vent smoker chimneys were sawed off the seafloor and brought to the surface. The chimneys had formed in water about 2,700 meters (about 8,900 feet) deep. Some were still hot inside. Microbiologists found even more bacteria in the chimney's walls that can live at temperatures higher than the boiling point of water at the surface. These bacteria may help answer an important question about all life—what is the highest temperature at which living things can survive?

The Ancient Archaea

Microbiologists—scientists who study the tiniest living things—think that even though archaea look just like bacteria, they are "as different from bacteria as bacteria are from trees," according to Carl Wirsen. These small and primitive organisms that sometimes live at high temperatures and without oxygen may be similar to the earliest forms of life on our planet.

This picture, magnified 10,000 times, shows archaea (the small circles) on a piece of the inside of a hot smoker chimney.

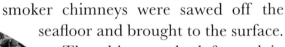

Archaea are the small white circles.

Microbiologist Andreas Teske (right) examines bacteria-containing vent deposits with Holger Jannasch aboard ship.

Working Together

Few scientists get a chance to go on a research cruise to the vents, and fewer still get a chance to dive in *Alvin*. The submersible has room for only two scientists on a dive, but there are scientists interested in biology, geology, chemistry, and other fields on the cruise. All of these scientists want to do many different kinds of experiments in *Alvin*. So they try to work together to meet everyone's needs.

"The thing that's difficult is that because there are only two of you in the sub, and a vent is such a multidisciplinary place, you're trying to collect what other people need as well," says geochemist Susan Humphris. "You're trying to remember everything everybody told you about. Well, exactly where did they want the temperature measurement to be taken? How am I supposed to collect the fluid? Am I remembering to do this right? What type of rock did they want from here? You're really trying to do your best to make sure everybody's getting what they want, so you won't go back to the surface and they'll say, 'Where's my temperature measurement from outside the chimney?' and you have to say 'Oops! I knocked the chimney over!' It's a big responsibility when you dive. You're trying to do what you need, and you're also trying to do the best you can for everybody else."

Why is this question important? One reason is that scientists think that conditions at the vents may be similar to the conditions that existed in our planet's very early history. At the time when life began on Earth, temperatures were extremely hot, and there was little oxygen. Both of these conditions are good for vent archaea. WHOI microbiologist Andreas Teske thinks that some of the vent archaea may be closely related to the first types of life on Earth. He searches for microorganisms in the warm mud and rocks below the seafloor of vent areas. The microorganisms he finds are often archaea. Understanding archaea could help scientists understand the beginnings of life on Earth—and elsewhere.

The most surprising new vent research may not even be on this planet. One of Jupiter's moons, Europa, appears to have an ice-covered ocean and active volcanoes. There might even be hydrothermal vents. Could there be life under the ice? Scientists like Andreas think there could be, and U.S. National Aeronautics and Space Administration (NASA) agrees. A group of scientists and engineers are beginning to work together to design equipment that could search for life beneath Europa's ice.

The first step, Andreas says, is to build something that can go below the surface of an ice-covered lake, such as a lake in Antarctica, and release a small robot to look for bacteria. This robot would have to be able to work in extreme cold. But scientists' experience tells them that hydrothermal vents can be very hot. So any equipment used to explore Europa has to work in both very cold and very hot

Images of Europa sent back from NASA's *Galileo* spacecraft on a mission to Jupiter support the theory that slush or even liquid may be found under the surface of this moon. In this image Europa's water-ice crust can be seen clearly. The lines on Europa's surface are large fractures, or cracks, in the ice.

The surface of Europa may be similar to that of this ice-covered lake in Antarctica. Scientists hope to discover whether there is life under Europa's ice.

environments. "It has to be prepared for everything," says Andreas. "It has to be prepared for all forms of microbial life, including forms we don't know. That's really difficult."

Whatever discoveries lie ahead on other planets, we have already discovered alien places in our own world, under our seas. At first sight, hydrothermal vents were the strangest places imaginable. Their discovery overturned ideas about the deep sea and life there. Patient work by many people in different places has explained much about what hydrothermal vent communities are and why they can exist.

Learning about these extraordinary ecosystems has led to a greater understanding of global geology. Hydrothermal vent research is also leading the way to knowing more about the extent, limits, and possible origins of life. The vents, says geochemist Susan Humphris, "demonstrate very clearly the interconnectedness of physics, chemistry, biology, and geology." And the more scientists can connect pieces of the vent puzzle, the better picture we will have of our planet and how it works. There is definitely more to discover at the bottom of the sunless sea.

Hydrothermal vents still hold many secrets. New vent sites, new mysteries, and new discoveries lie deep beneath the surface of all the world's oceans.

Dan Fornari has been fascinated by vents throughout his career. He says, "They embody so much of what we understand to be the dynamic Earth." He is shown here looking at a section of a vent chimney.

GLOSSARY

antibiotic A compound that kills bacteria, especially a compound produced by living organisms that, when taken by people, helps them fight off infections.

archaea [ar-KEE-ah] A type of very small microorganism that is very different from bacteria and may be similar to the earliest forms of life.

biologist A scientist who studies living things and the types and processes of life.

chemosynthesis [KEY-moe-SIN-the-sis] A process in which bacteria get energy for growth from inorganic chemicals such as hydrogen sulfide, iron, or ammonia.

chlorophyll [KLOR-a-fil] A green compound produced by plants that absorbs light energy and enables the plant to use the energy to grow.

colony A group of organisms of identical genetic makeup that live together, either physically or socially, as one organism. Corals are colonial animals; ants and bees form social colonies.

consumer An organism that eats plants, eats other animals, or obtains food from chemosynthetic bacteria.

dissolve To come apart and disperse into a liquid in such a way that the molecules of the solid are completely surrounded by the liquid.

DNA Deoxyribonucleic acid. The molecules, found in the nucleus of cells, that contain the genetic code of most organisms.

ecologist A scientist who studies living things in relation to each other and to their environment.

ecosystem The living and nonliving things that interact with each other in an environment.

geochemist A scientist who specializes in the study of the chemical properties of compounds that make up the earth and sea.

geologist A scientist who studies the earth's structure, composition, and history.

geyser A vent or opening in the earth from which water and steam periodically erupt into the air. Underground water contacts hot rocks, generating steam and building up pressure that is released when the geyser erupts and water shoots out.

hemoglobin [HEE-ma-glo-bin] A red-pigmented compound in the blood of many animals that bonds to oxygen, carrying it through the animal's bloodstream and releasing it to the animal's cells.

hydrogen sulfide An inorganic compound made of one sulfur atom and two hydrogen atoms. Hydrogen sulfide is poisonous to most living organisms.

hydrothermal Having to do with hot water. Hydrothermal vents are openings in the seafloor from which flows hot water mixed with chemicals.

metal ores Naturally occurring minerals from which metals can be extracted by heating or other processes.

microbiologist A biologist who studies microscopic living things, particularly bacteria.

microorganisms Very small living cells, too small to be seen without a microscope.

photosynthesis The process by which green plants get energy for growth from sunlight, carbon dioxide (from the air), and water to make sugars.

precipitation The process of becoming solid by coming out of a dissolved state and forming solid pieces or particles that settle out of the surrounding liquid.

primary producer A living organism (usually a plant) that produces organic matter from inorganic matter and energy sources.

shimmering water Warm vent fluid mixed with seawater that seeps up through cracks in the lava around a vent area. The water is warm when it enters cold seawater, so heat distortions form.

sulfur An element common in volcanic material, either in yellow crystals of pure sulfur or as part of other minerals or compounds.

symbiosis [sim-bee-OH-sis] A partnership between two organisms in which both benefit.

volcanic Having to do with the emergence of steam and gases and the flow of molten rock from below the earth's surface.

wavelength In light, a property that we see as color. Different colors have different wavelengths, red being the longest and violet the shortest.

FURTHER READING

Dipper, Francis. *Mysteries of the Ocean Deep.* New York: Copper Beech, 1996.

Gowell, Elizabeth Tayntor. *Fountains of Life: The Story of Deep-Sea Vents.* Danbury, CT: Franklin Watts, 1998.

Johnson, Rebecca L. *Diving into Darkness: A Submersible Explores the Sea.* Chicago: Lerner, 1989.

Kovacs, Deborah. *Dive to the Deep Ocean: Voyages of Exploration and Discovery.* Austin, TX: Raintree/Steck-Vaughn, 2000.

Kovacs, Deborah, and Kate Madin. *Beneath Blue Waters: Meetings with Remarkable Deep-Sea Creatures.* New York: Viking, 1996.

Taylor, Leighton R. *Creeps from the Deep: Life in the Deep Sea.* San Francisco: Chronicle Books, 1997.

Van Dover, Cindy Lee. *Deep-Ocean Journeys: Discovering New Life at the Bottom of the Sea.* New York: Perseus Books, 1997.

INDEX

Acknowledgments

I'd like to thank the many people at WHOI and elsewhere who helped make this book possible. First, my thanks go to the people I interviewed and who very kindly read the manuscript: Colleen Cavanaugh, Jack Donnelly, Dan Fornari, Ken Halanych, Bob Hessler, Susan Humphris, Steve Molyneaux, Lauren Mullineaux, Andreas Teske, Meg Tivey, Cindy Van Dover, Dick Von Herzen, and Carl Wirsen. My thanks also go to those who helped me find photographs and materials: Shelley Lauzon, Kathy Patterson, and Tom Kleindinst. Thanks especially to Deborah Kovacs, who was a supportive friend and colleague throughout, and to Audrey Bryant, who worked closely, kindly, and carefully with me as editor. Grateful thanks to Larry Madin and Judy McDowell, who helped in so many ways. And heartfelt gratitude to Holger Jannasch, who generously shared his time, knowledge, and enthusiasm for microbiology and for the teaching of science, in a lengthy interview in the summer of 1998.

Credits

All photographs courtesy of Woods Hole Oceanographic Institution (WHOI), except for the following:

Aubrey, Steve/WHOI: 58–59; Brenner, Dave/University of Alaska Sea Grant: 14, 44, 45, back cover; Childress, Jim/University of California at Santa Barbara: 37 bottom; Deep Submergence Operations Group/WHOI: 1, 1 inset, 5, 6, 9, 10 bottom, 21, 23, 36 bottom, 37 top; Dickson, Craig/WHOI: 41, 55; Donnelly, Jack/WHOI: 15 left; Edmond, John/Massachusetts Institute of Technology: 22 bottom; Fornari, Dan/WHOI: 33 bottom; Fornari, Dan and Rachel Haymon/WHOI: 17, 24 top; Foster, Dudley/WHOI: 15 right; Grassle, J. Frederick/WHOI: 2 left; Hamilton, Calvin/Jet Propulsion Lab, NASA: 57; Hessler, Robert/Scripps Institute of Oceanography: 12; Humphris, Susan/WHOI: 22 top; Jannasch, Holger/WHOI: 18; Kleindinst, Tom/WHOI: 28, 52, 59 bottom inset; Molyneaux, Steve/WHOI: 42; Mullineaux, Lauren/WHOI: 4, 11 top; National Geographic Society: 16 right, 34; Ripley, Bonnie: 38 bottom; Peter Rona/National Oceanic and Atmospheric Administration: 16 left; Shank, Tim/Rutgers University and WHOI: 53; Spindell, Robert/WHOI: 43; Sulanowska, Margaret/WHOI: 56; Thompson, Geoffrey/WHOI: 39 bottom; United States Geological Survey: 8, 40; Whitehead, Jack/WHOI: 13; Wirsen, Carl/WHOI: 26, 27, 30, 32, 33 top, 36 top, 49, 54; Wirsen, Carl and Steve Molyneaux/WHOI: 42.

Illustrations on pages 7, 20, 29, 46, and 50–51 are by Patricia Wynne.